WATER, WATER!

Water, water everywhere and lots of it to drink.
This American girl drinks from a water fountain.

No water, no water, no clean water can be found.
This Congolese boy has to drink dirty water from the lake.

No taps in the house, no taps in the village. These African boys pump their water up from a well.

They use wells in Morocco, too. These children are filling lots of bottles – enough water to last for days.

A big pot of water for cleaning food and cooking in.
In Brazil a family prepares cassavas for tea.

Time to wash up! In Burkina Faso a special sink has been built in the river to keep the animals out.

Water for keeping clean, water for washing clothes and water for the dishes. Here in Nepal everyone is hard at work.

In Cameroon a mother washes her clothes in the river – and baby comes along for a paddle, too!

Crying and shouting won't do any good. It's time to get washed in the Congo and that means the baby, too.

In some parts of China the houses have no bathrooms
so this boy brushes his teeth out on the street.

Have you ever rowed to the shops before? In this market in Thailand the boats are the shops – they sell food of every kind.

In New Guinea it's raining and it's pouring and there's no roof on the boat! Lucky these boys have a palm leaf to shelter from the storm.

I spy a fish from high up on these poles. These Sri Lankan fishermen are trying to catch their lunch.

With his net like a pocket on poles this French fisherman hopes to catch himself some shrimp.

In Mali the ground is dry and there isn't a cloud in the sky. Carefully the farmer waters his plants and hopes the rain comes soon.

When there's plenty of rain it's easy to water plants – in the United Kingdom great sprinklers shoot water far across the fields.

Rice needs lots of water if it's going to survive, so in China they plant it in curved pools of water stacked one above another.

Pools of water in Peru, too; but not for growing plants.

Here they are drying seawater to harvest all the salt.

Imagine a city with no cars. Welcome to Venice in Italy, where the roads are canals – you can catch a boat to get around.

Houses built on water standing on stilts to keep them dry.
This town in Malaysia is built over a lake.

Heavy rain, monsoon rain – it's a day for staying under cover in Bangladesh.

The waters have risen too far and flooded the town. These French people have found their street is now a river.

Here in Ethiopia a man watches his lands turn into a desert.
The rain hasn't come and everything has died.

Even when there's plenty of water it is sometimes hard to find. In Patagonia the water is hidden under the ice and snow.

Water can be fun to play in. Here in Hawaii, big waves mean big fun for this windsurfer.

Under the waves around the Marshall Islands lie colourful coral gardens for these divers to explore.

What could be more fun than splashing around in the water?
These children in Laos can't think of anything better!